Discovering
Cultures
China

Sandy Asher

BENCHMARK **B**OOKS

MARSHALL CAVENDISH
NEW YORK

With thanks to Heather Clydesdale, M. Phil in Chinese Art History, Columbia University and former Assistant Director of Curriculum Development, Asia Society, for the careful review of this manuscript.

Acknowledgments

My thanks to the following people for their generous help: Ben Asher, Harvey Asher, Hue-Ping Chin of Drury University's Interdisciplinary Studies Department, Li Ruifang and Wang Ying of Tsinghua University's Department of Foreign Languages, and Mingzheng Shi, East Asia Regional Director, Council on International Educational Exchange. *Xiexie!*

Benchmark Books
Marshall Cavendish
99 White Plains Road, Tarrytown, New York 10591-9001
Text copyright © 2003 by Marshall Cavendish Corporation
Map and illustrations copyright © 2003 by Marshall Cavendish Corporation
Map and illustrations by Salvatore Murdocca
Book design by Virginia Pope

Library of Congress Cataloging-in-Publication Data

Asher, Sandy.
China / by Sandy Asher.
p. cm. — (Discovering cultures)
Includes bibliographical references and index.
Summary: An introduction to China, highlighting the country's geography, people, foods, schools, recreation, celebrations, and language.
ISBN 0-7614-1179-8
1. China—Juvenile literature. [1. China.] I. Title. II. Series.
DS706 .A84 2002
951—dc21   2001007293

Photo Research by Candlepants Incorporated
Cover Photo: Corbis/Dean Conger

The photographs in this book are used by permission and through the courtesy of; Corbis: John Slater, 1, 12, 34; Todd Gipstein, 4-5, 20 (left); Dean Conger, 6; Eye Ubiquitous, 8,10; Liu Liqun, 9, 15, 37 ; Keren Su,11, 25 (lower), 31, 32, 34-35, 40 ; Dallas and John Heaton, 13, 28 ; Bohemien Nomad Picturemakers, 14; Joseph Sohm/Chromosohm Inc., 16, 26; Wolfgang Kaehler, 17; Tom Nebbia,19; Vince Streano, 20 (right); Arne Hodalic, 21; Michael S. Yamashita, 22, 25 (top); Neveda Wier, 24; Reed Kaestner, 30; Phil Meister, 36; Jack Fields, 38-39; Wally McNamee, 44 (left); Christies Images, 45; Dave Bartruff, back cover. Albert Lee: 18, 29. Getty One/FPG/Keren Su: 44 (right).

Cover: *The Great Wall of China*; Title page: *A Spring Festival dancer wearing a mask*

Printed in Hong Kong

1 3 5 6 4 2

Turn the Pages...

Nǐ hǎo!

That's Chinese for hello.

At times in its long history, China has seemed closed to the rest of the world. But through the years, it has shared its rich culture with many countries.

What is China like today?

Let's find out...

A Chinese student wearing her school uniform

Where in the World Is China?

Stretching across eastern Asia, China is home to more than one billion people. No country has more citizens. It is the third largest country in the world. Only Russia and Canada cover more land.

Mountains and desert make up two-thirds of China. Because they are difficult to climb and cross, they have protected the country from invaders. But they also leave

A farmer hoes a field at the foot of a mountain.

Tian Shan

Beijing ★

Huang He

Yellow Sea

Shanghai

Chāng Jiāng

N
NW   NE
W   E
SW   SE
S

Tourists travel down the Yellow River on a raft.

very little land for farming, less than 20 percent. That's not much land to feed so many people.

In the northwest, there are mountains covered with snow. Rivers cut through them, and a mist rises that makes their peaks seem to float. These mountains are called Tian Shan, or Celestial Mountains. Celestial means heavenly.

Northeastern China is very cold in winter. The people who live there cut blocks of ice from the river and create beautiful ice sculptures. This area is rich in coal and other minerals and has large industries.

Some of China's most fertile farmland is in the north, along the Huang He, or Yellow River, named for its muddy color. As the Huang He flows east toward the

Yellow Sea, it deposits rich soil along its banks. There, farmers raise soybeans, wheat, barley, fruits, cotton, and other crops.

The Huang He is sometimes called the River of Sorrow. Its many floods have swept away entire villages. Dams and canals now help control the floods.

China's capital city, Beijing, is in northern China. It is the country's second largest city, with ten million people.

The Chāng Jǐang, or Long River, marks the boundary between northern and southern China. Like the Huang He, the Chāng Jǐang provides fertile soil but also causes life-threatening floods. It flows over 3,000 miles (4,828 kilometers) and is the third longest river in the world.

Shanghai, in the south, is China's largest city, with more than 13 million people. A busy seaport for 150 years, it is also an important educational and industrial center.

Crowds of people and bright lights fill Shanghai at night.

Southern China is very warm. Farming goes on year round. Rice is the area's most important crop. But nature turns dangerous here, too. During the summer monsoon season, huge rainstorms blow in from the sea.

The people of China feel close to nature. They celebrate it in their festivals, paintings, and poems. In the eighth century, the poet Li Bo wrote, "This is a special, beautiful place." His words are still true.

Rice fields beside a river village

The Giant Panda

China is the only place in the world where giant pandas live in the wild. And the cool, misty mountain forests of the southwest are the only place in China they can be found. That's where bamboo trees grow. Although giant pandas will eat other plants, bamboo is their favorite food.

Chinese books written more than three thousand years ago mention the giant panda. Giant pandas were also once kept as pets by Chinese emperors. Many people believed that these unusual creatures had magical powers and brought good luck.

Once plentiful, the giant panda is now one of the rarest animals in the world. There are probably fewer than a thousand left in the wild. In recent years, they have had to compete for space with farmers who need the river valleys and the lower slopes of the mountains to grow crops.

The giant panda has become a world-famous symbol of endangered species everywhere. The Chinese government is working with organizations in the United States and elsewhere to preserve this national treasure.

What Makes China Chinese?

Throughout history, China has seen many changes in its people and their daily lives. More than 90 percent of the Chinese belong to an ethnic group known as Han. But there are people from other ethnic groups in China as well, including Uighurs, Manchurians, and Mongolians. While mandarin Chinese is the official language, many dialects are spoken in different parts of the country.

In English, this vast country's full name is the People's Republic of China. The Chinese also refer to their country as Zhōngguó. That means the middle kingdom. China was ruled by emperors for thousands of years. Some of them thought of their kingdom as the center of the world. Under their rule, few Chinese traveled to other countries, and foreigners were rarely allowed to visit. Long walls were built to keep out invaders. The Great Wall located north of Beijing is the most famous.

A Han Chinese boy

The Great Wall of China curves across the mountains.

The emperors believed that beyond their borders people were not civilized. And, indeed, China was far ahead in many things, including science and arts and crafts. The Chinese invented the first compass, discovered medicines to treat asthma and other illnesses, and tracked comets across the sky. Statues, paintings, and pottery created in China over the past five thousand years are still highly admired.

Today, China touches our lives in many ways. We eat Chinese food. We even use cups, saucers, and plates that are sometimes called china. That's because they are often made of porcelain, a Chinese invention. We practice *kung fu* and other Chinese martial arts. We fly kites, shoot off fireworks, and use umbrellas, silk, and paper money— all Chinese inventions.

An ancient statue stands guard in a park.

Exploring the Internet at a computer club

China also plays an important role in the world's politics and economy. Its decisions about trade, security, and the environment affect us all.

Modern Chinese life includes inventions that come from the United States and other countries. The largest cities bustle with tourists, and are filled with televisions, computers, skyscrapers, superhighways, and dozens of McDonald's restaurants!

An early visit to China in the year 1271 became famous throughout Europe. An Italian merchant named Marco Polo traveled east from Venice, Italy, to a land he knew as Cathay. There he found an advanced civilization whose inventions and

Reading the menu at a Chinese McDonald's in Beijing

discoveries amazed him. Some say Marco Polo brought Chinese noodles back to Italy, where they were later called spaghetti.

Chinese food is now popular in many countries, but restaurants sometimes change their recipes to suit local tastes. Chop suey, chow mein, and fortune cookies, for instance, were all created in the United States.

The people of modern China welcome visitors to their homeland. They also travel to other countries to visit, study, and perform. Perhaps you have watched Chinese athletes compete in the Olympics. Or maybe you have admired the amazing feats of Chinese acrobats and jugglers.

Though our countries influence one another, there are things that belong to China and no place else. Nature, history, language, and tradition have made this country unique.

Chinese Calligraphy

Calligraphy means good writing, and good writing, or penmanship, has been a highly respected art in China for many centuries.

It takes years of practice to learn how to do Chinese calligraphy well. There are thousands of characters in the Chinese language. Each of these characters represents a word.

The calligrapher uses special materials for this art form. Brushes, pens, ink, and paper are chosen carefully. Chinese ink comes in dry sticks. The calligrapher puts water into a flat ink-stone and then grinds the stick of ink against the stone to get the right shade.

Modern Chinese people write from the left side of the page to the right. But calligraphers follow the old tradition of writing in columns from the top of each page to the bottom, and from the right side to the left. All of the characters are created out of just seven basic brush strokes. An experienced calligrapher can do the strokes so quickly that onlookers sometimes say he is using a "flying brush."

Living in China

China is such a big country that life in one area is different from life in another. In Beijing and other cities, many families live in tall apartment buildings. The streets are always crowded with people, bicycles, cars, buses, and trucks. There are lots of

People and vehicles clog a busy city street.

Some families live on houseboats in the country.

modern offices, restaurants, hotels, and stores. In the countryside, most houses are small. They may be built around a courtyard shared with other families. Nearly two-thirds of the people in China are farmers. Modern farming equipment is becoming more common, but much of the work is still done by hand and with simple tools.

In spite of these differences, some things are the same throughout China. The People's Republic of China has been a Communist country since 1949. Communists believe that people should work for the good of the community. All land and public buildings are owned by the state. But the idea of free trade is spreading quickly. Farmers, for instance, are now allowed to sell some of their crops on their own. These and many other goods can be found at roadside stands and outdoor markets.

Family life has always been important in China. In most families, fathers and mothers both work. Grandparents often help take care of the children.

Fresh produce for sale at an outdoor market

Tea is the traditional drink all over China, but each region has its own style of cooking. In the north, there isn't enough rain to grow rice, so most dishes are made from wheat flour. Northern Chinese eat lots of noodles and dumplings. The northern style of cooking is called Beijing or mandarin.

Spicy dishes made with hot peppers, green onions, and ginger are eaten in the Sichuan province. The Chāng Jiǎng and the hot, humid climate make this area perfect for growing rice.

Grandparents are an important part of a Chinese family.

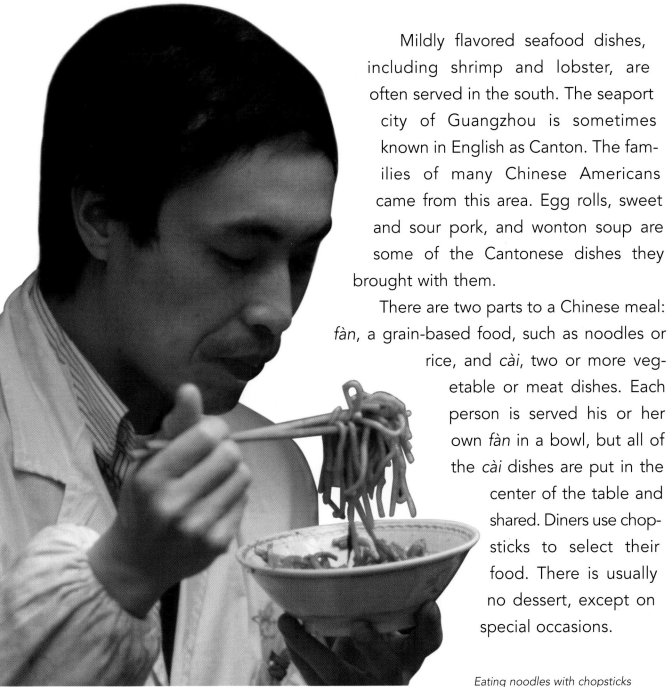

Mildly flavored seafood dishes, including shrimp and lobster, are often served in the south. The seaport city of Guangzhou is sometimes known in English as Canton. The families of many Chinese Americans came from this area. Egg rolls, sweet and sour pork, and wonton soup are some of the Cantonese dishes they brought with them.

There are two parts to a Chinese meal: *fàn*, a grain-based food, such as noodles or rice, and *cài*, two or more vegetable or meat dishes. Each person is served his or her own *fàn* in a bowl, but all of the *cài* dishes are put in the center of the table and shared. Diners use chopsticks to select their food. There is usually no dessert, except on special occasions.

Eating noodles with chopsticks

There are many dishes to choose from at this family dinner.

No matter where they live, Chinese cooks like to prepare their meals from fresh ingredients every day. And families like to eat together. Good food and good manners are always expected at the table.

Let's Eat!
Egg Drop Soup

This soup is also called Egg Flower Soup because of the designs made by the strands of egg. It is a good last-minute recipe, often made only with water, green onions, and eggs. It is quick and easy, but make sure you ask an adult to help. You can use canned broth for the stock.

Ingredients:

1 quart chicken or
vegetable stock

2 green onions (scallions),
chopped into thin rings

A large handful of lettuce or spinach leaves,
washed and shredded into long strands

2 eggs, beaten well

1 teaspoon sesame
or vegetable oil

Salt and pepper

Wash your hands. Stir the salt and pepper into the beaten eggs. Set aside. Heat the stock in a saucepan, but do not boil. Add the scallions and shredded leaves and stir until they wilt. Bring the soup to a boil and stir in the oil. Add the eggs, pouring them into the soup in a thin, steady stream. Let the eggs set for just a few seconds, then stir the soup briskly with a fork until they become frilly strands.
Serves four.

School Days

Students in China learn to study hard, to be polite and honest, and to respect one another and their elders.

Many toddlers attend nursery school while their parents are at work. Even though they are young, they learn to be helpful. A nursery school in the countryside might raise a pig to teach children how to take care of animals. Like nursery school students around the world, they also sing songs, play games, and listen to stories.

At age six or seven, children begin elementary school. They attend classes five days a week. Their studies include citizenship, Chinese language, arithmetic, science, history, geography, physical education, and the arts. Some also learn English, Russian, or Japanese.

Children in the early grades spend nearly half their school day learning to read and write Chinese. That's because words in Chinese must be learned by heart. They cannot be sounded out like English because each word is represented by its own special character. Elementary school children need to memorize about

At school in the countryside

three thousand characters. That can take four years!

A modern system called Pinyin has made learning the language easier. Students begin by using Roman letters, the same alphabet we use to read and write English. That way, they can sound out written words. Later, they learn the Chinese character for each word.

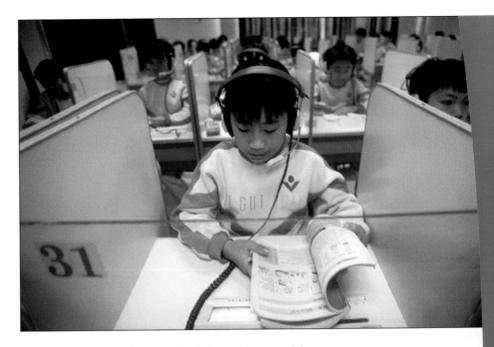

Learning English at a language lab

In the cities, children who show talent in sports, art, music, math, science, or other areas may attend classes in these subjects after school. There are also special schools for very talented children. Gymnasts, for instance, may begin their training as young as three years old. Part of their day is spent on regular studies. The rest is spent practicing their skills.

At about age twelve, children take an exam to go on to middle school. Later, those who want

A young gymnast practices her handstand.

to continue their education will take more exams to enter high school and college. These exams are very competitive.

Students who do not go to college may be trained in factory skills. In the countryside, young people learn to do farm work.

The school year in China includes twelve weeks of vacation. Like children all over the world, Chinese students work hard in school—and enjoy their days off!

Schoolboys enjoy a field trip

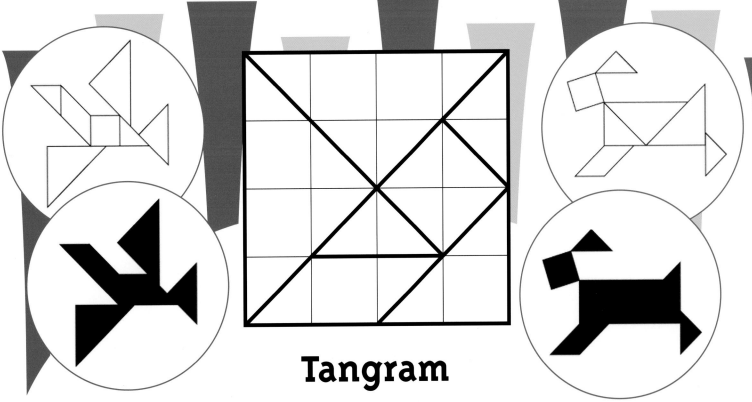

Tangram

A tangram is a Chinese game, puzzle, and art, craft, and math lesson all rolled into one! Tangrams are made up of seven shapes called *tans*. The *tans* include five triangles, one square, and one rhomboid. Tangram sets may be made out of paper, cardboard, wood, glass, or any other material that can be cut into perfect geometric shapes.

Make your own tangram set:

1. Using a ruler and pencil, draw a large, perfect square on colored paper, four inches on each side.

2. Divide your large square into sixteen smaller squares, one inch on each side.

3. Use the squares as guidelines to draw the seven geometric shapes, as shown above.

4. Carefully cut out the seven shapes, or *tans*—five triangles, one square, and one rhomboid.

5. Arrange the *tans* to create tangrams. First, copy the pictures shown, then make up your own! The *tans* should touch one another, but not overlap.

Experts have created thousands of tangrams: people, animals, objects, letters, and numbers. How many can you make out of your seven *tans*?

Just for Fun

How do Chinese children spend their free time? They may play games, watch TV, go to the movies, or visit relatives and friends.

Buildings crowd the Forbidden City

Inside one of the Forbidden City's many rooms

On sunny days in the city, there is a lot to see and do in the park. Shadowboxers practice their skills. Bands play, and couples dance. Vendors sell toys, souvenirs, and ice cream from their stalls. Calligraphers and painters display their art. Everywhere you look, people walk, talk, ride bicycles, or sit and sip tea.

The capital city of Beijing is China's most popular tourist spot. Visitors have a choice of dozens of museums and one of the world's largest zoos.

Every year, millions of people visit the Palace Museum in a section of Beijing known as the Forbidden City. The Forbidden City was the home of China's emperors from 1403 until 1912. A sprawling village with 9,999 rooms and halls, it was closed for hundreds of years to everyone except royalty, officials, and their servants.

A day at the beach

There is much to see outside of Beijing as well. Thousands of tourists, Chinese and foreign, stroll the Great Wall every day. Many go mountain climbing or visit the beautiful gardens at Suzhou. In the summer, the ocean is a popular vacation spot.

Playing Ping-Pong

Sports are enjoyed all over China. Ping-Pong, or table tennis, is a favorite. There are local and national competitions every year. The Chinese also enjoy watching soccer, basketball, track and field, baseball, and football. Their Olympic teams always bring home medals, especially in gymnastics, swimming, diving, table tennis, and judo.

The martial arts are an important form of exercise in China. Some, such as *kung fu*, are very tough. Others, such as Taijiquan, are more gentle. Taijiquan's slow movements teach balance and control. They are very graceful and are meant to resemble floating clouds and running water. Every morning, Chinese people of all ages practice Taijiquan. Exercise, art, and nature blend together to begin the new day.

Kung fu requires strength and flexibility.

Tiao Fangzi

A kind of Chinese hopscotch, Tiao Fangzi is a game for two
or more players. The name means "hopping house."

1. Draw a large rectangle on the sidewalk with chalk. Divide it into eight
smaller spaces, as shown.

2. Number the small spaces 1 to 7, and mark the last space "Public House."

3. The first player drops a stone in the first space, then hops in, picks it up, throws it out,
and hops back out. This must all be done
on one foot, without stepping on a line.

4. If the player succeeds, he or she drops the
stone into the second space, hops into
spaces one and two, picks up the stone,
throws it out, and hops back out again.

5. The first player keeps going until he or she
picks up the stone in all seven spaces. The
Public House is a place to rest. Players
may put both feet down in this space.

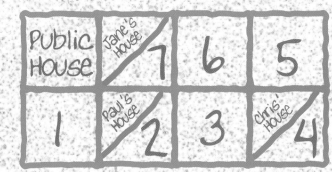

6. If the first player does step on a line or put down his or her raised foot in any other
space, it is the next player's turn.

7. When a player completes all seven spaces without missing, he or she draws a
line to mark off half of any space and writes his or her name inside. This is
a Private House, and it's a resting place for that player only. Others
who step inside or drop the stone there lose their turn.

8. The player with the most Private Houses at the
end of the game wins.

Let's Celebrate!

Fireworks, drums, and sweet cakes! Chinese holidays are feasts for the eyes, ears, and taste buds.

The new year begins with Spring Festival. Outside of China, this holiday is often called Chinese New Year. It is also known as the Lunar New Year. Chinese holidays usually follow the old lunar calendar. Lunar refers to the moon. Each month of the lunar calendar begins with a new moon.

Spring Festival is a time for fresh starts and family reunions. As winter and the old year end, everyone cleans house, puts on fine clothes, and goes visiting. Doorways are decorated with poems and pictures of flowers and birds. Windows and doors may also get a fresh coat of paint.

A Spring Festival dancer

The Dragon Dance is a Spring Festival tradition.

A gift of lucky money

Families and friends gather for meals, exchange gifts, and wish each other good luck in the new year. The color red is a Chinese symbol of good luck. During Spring Festival, children are given bright red envelopes that contain "lucky money." Dragons and dancers in lion masks also bring good luck as they parade down the street. In northern China, good luck dumplings are served. All over the country, fireworks are set off for days.

Fifteen days after Spring Festival, the first full moon of the year appears. Now it is time for the Lantern Festival. Displaying lanterns is a Chinese custom

Colorful lanterns on display

that goes back thousands of years. Today, city and village streets are strung with lanterns of all sizes and shapes. Sweet cakes, fireworks, stilt walkers, and folk dancers add to the fun.

Later in the spring, during Clear and Bright Festival people pay respect to the dead but also celebrate the coming of spring. They may visit family graves and the tombs of national heroes. They may also go to a park to enjoy a stroll on the new spring grass and fly a kite. All over China, the sky fills with beautifully decorated kites, flown by young and old alike.

The Dragon Boat Festival falls on the fifth day of the

A flying dragon kite

fifth lunar month, sometime in May or June. It honors the poet Qu Yuan, who lived almost 2,500 years ago. People row dragon boats on the rivers in his honor, racing to the sounds of beating drums and cheering crowds.

Mid-autumn Festival is a very old holiday and a time for family reunions. Families sit outside together enjoying the brightest full moon of the year and sharing specially baked moon cakes. People who are far away from their families look up at the moon and think of their loved ones.

Throughout the year, the people of China have a great deal to celebrate!

Racing a dragon boat

High on a mountain, long ago,
there lived a terrible beast named Nian—or so the legend
tells us. At the end of every year, this beast would come down from its
mountaintop and kill animals and people. At last, people learned that Nian was
afraid of noise and light. At the end of the next year, they set off fireworks! The beast
was so frightened, it ran until its head fell off. Fireworks have welcomed the Lunar New
Year ever since. *Nián* is the Chinese word for year.

Two Spring Festival Stories

It is said that during the Tang Dynasty (618–906), the emperor of China
fell ill. In his restless dreams, he heard the howling of ghosts. Eager to help him,
two of his generals began standing guard each night outside his door. The dreams
stopped. The emperor was grateful, but thought it unfair to ask the generals to go on
standing guard every night. So he ordered his artists to paint pictures of the generals
and hang them on his doors as Door Gods. The emperor and his generals slept
well, and the ghosts howled no more. Today Chinese people still
hang pictures of Door Gods on their doorways during
Spring Festival.

The red background of the Chinese flag stands for the revolution. The large yellow star represents the Communist Party. The four smaller stars show the people of China united under one government.

Chinese money is called yuan. The exchange rate often changes, but currently one American dollar equals 8.28 yuan.

Count in Chinese

English	Chinese	Say it like this:
one	yī	YEE
two	èr	UHR
three	sān	SAHN
four	sì	SER
five	wǔ	WOO
six	liù	LYOO
seven	qī	CHEE
eight	bā	BAH
nine	jiǔ	jee-OO
ten	shí	SHER

Glossary

Chāng Jǐang (CHAANG CHEE-ang)   River dividing northern and southern China.

dialect   Unique way a language is spoken in a particular region.

Huang He (HWANG HUH)   River in Northern China, also known as the Yellow River.

lunar month   Begins with the new moon and lasts for 29 to 30 days, until the next new moon appears.

mandarin   The style of cooking in Beijing and the most common Chinese language.

monsoon   Strong summer wind in Southern Asia, and the rains that come with it.

nǐ hǎo (NEE ha-OW)   Hello in Chinese.

Pinyin   Method of teaching Chinese by spelling out words by their sounds.

republic   Country in which the people elect their government representatives.

Proud to Be Chinese

Kongfuzi, also called Confucius (551 B.C.E.–447 B.C.E.)

This wise man and teacher was born in the state of Lu, before China was a unified country. It was a time when many powerful men fought for control of the land and people. Kongfuzi believed in studying history to find the best way things were done in the past, and then using that knowledge to improve the present. He taught that strong families were the basis for strong communities, and that each person should do what is best for the family and the community. His ideas have long been a part of Chinese life.

Lu Chen (1976–   )

Figure skater Lu Chen was born in Jilin, China. Lulu, as she is sometimes called, began skating on a frozen field at the age of four. She wore second-hand boys' skates that had to be stuffed with socks because they were too large. Ice-skating was not a popular sport in China at the time, so rinks and equipment were hard to find. Lulu began competing at age fourteen. In 1994, she became the first Chinese skater to win an Olympic medal. In 1995, she was the first Chinese skater to win a world gold medal. In 1998, she began living and training in San Francisco. A popular performer in ice shows, Lulu has inspired young skaters in China and around the world.

Qi Baishi (1864–1957)

One of the most popular of China's ink-and-wash painters, Qi Baishi was born into a family of poor rice farmers in Xiangtan, Hunan Province. He had very little formal schooling as a child. His grandfather taught him to read and write. Qi Baishi began to study painting and calligraphy when he was twenty-four years old. Traditional Chinese ink-and-wash painting is very difficult to do well. The artist paints from memory, using special paper, a soft brush, and ink to capture the spirit of the object being painted. Once a stroke is made, it is never changed. Qi Baishi enjoyed painting animals, insects, and flowers. He continued to learn and perfect his painting all his life.

Find Out More

Books

China: The Dragon Awakes by Tony Zurlo. Dillon Press, New York, 1994.

China: The People (revised edition) by Bobbie Kalman. Crabtree Publishing, New York, 2000.

Look What Came from China by Miles Harvey. Franklin Watts, Connecticut, 1998.

A Taste of China by Roz Denny. Raintree Steck-Vaughn, New York, 1994.

Web Sites

http://www.chinapage.com/china.html

Offers pages in Chinese and in English. Learn about dragons, calligraphy, poetry, history, and more.

http://www.childbook.com

A site dedicated to children's books, videos, CDs, and cassettes relating to China and Chinese culture. Songs and stories are available in Chinese, English, or both.

Videos

The Arts and Entertainment/History Channel has many videos about China, including *China's Forbidden City* and *Modern Marvels: The Great Wall of China*. Visit their site at **http://www.aetv.com**.

Index

Page numbers for illustrations are in **boldface.**

About the Author

Sandy Asher is the author of many books, stories, poems, and plays for young people. She loves to travel and counts her visit to China in 2001 as one of her most exciting trips ever. You can visit her Web page at:

http://mowrites4kids.drury.edu/authors/asher